World of Reptiles

Garter Snakes

by Matt Doeden

Consultants:
The Staff of Reptile Gardens
Rapid City, South Dakota

Mankato, Minnesota

j QL666.O636 D64 2005
Doeden, Matt.
Garter snakes
Mankato, Minn. : Capstone
Press, c2005.

Bridgestone Books are published by Capstone Press,
151 Good Counsel Drive, P.O. Box 669, Mankato, Minnesota 56002.
www.capstonepress.com

Library of Congress Cataloging-in-Publication Data
Doeden, Matt.
  Garter snakes / by Matt Doeden.
    p. cm.—(Bridgestone Books. World of reptiles)
  Includes bibliographical references and index.
  ISBN 0-7368-3732-9 (hardcover)
  1. Garter snakes—Juvenile literature. I. Title. II. Series: World of Reptiles.
QL666.O636D64 2005
597.96'2—dc22   2004013238

Editorial Credits

Heather Adamson, editor; Enoch Peterson, designer; Erin Scott, illustrator; Jo Miller, photo researcher;
    Scott Thoms, photo editor

Photo Credits

Allen Blake Sheldon, cover
Bill Beatty, 12
Bruce Coleman Inc./Ed. Degginger, 4; Lynn Stone, 6; Daniel J. Lyons, 16
David Liebman, 1
McDonald Wildlife Photography/Joe McDonald, 18
Photo Researchers Inc./SPL/Alan Sirulnikoff, 20
Visuals Unlimited/Bill Beatty, 10

1 2 3 4 5 6 10 09 08 07 06 05

Table of Contents

Garter Snakes

Watch for a ripple in the water along a creek bank. A garter snake may be hunting a frog. Garter snakes are the most common snakes found in North America.

Garter snakes are reptiles. They can't make their own body heat. They are **cold-blooded**. Reptiles also have scales and grow from eggs.

Garter snakes do not hurt people. Like racers and rat snakes, they have no **venom**. Garters can only catch small **prey**.

◀ Garter snakes often hunt frogs near water.

What Garter Snakes Look Like

Garter snakes got their name from the long stripes on their bodies. People thought the striped scale pattern looked like sock garters. Sock garters are stretchy bands of cloth. They are worn around the top of socks to keep them from slipping. Most garter snakes have yellow, green, or orange stripes.

Garter snakes are short and thin. Most adults are between 1 and 2 feet (0.3 and 0.6 meter) long. Some garter snakes can grow to 4 feet (1.2 meters) long.

◄ Most garters have three stripes. Sometimes the center stripe is a different color.

Garter Snakes Range Map

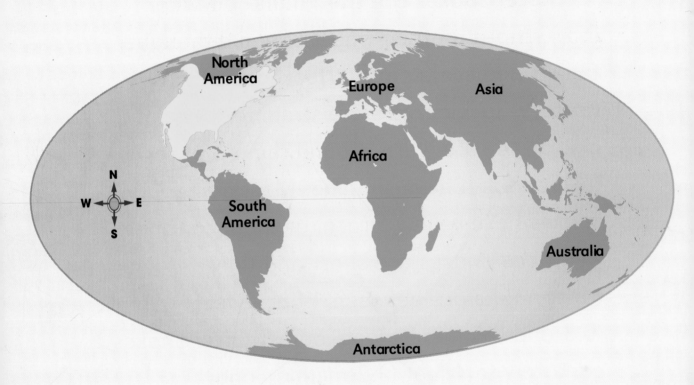

North America

Europe

Asia

Africa

South America

Australia

Antarctica

N
W — E
S

☐ Where Garter Snakes Live

Garter Snakes in the World

Garter snakes can live almost anywhere in North America except deserts. They can live in grasslands, woodlands, and even shady backyards.

Garter snakes are common in the United States and Canada. Garter snakes live as far north as Alaska and as far south as the Gulf of Mexico.

◄ Twenty-two different kinds of garter snakes live throughout North America.

Garter Snake Habitats

Garter snakes live in a wide range of habitats. Most garter snakes live in wet meadows or damp forests. They hunt prey that live in or near ponds, rivers, and lakes.

Garter snakes in cold areas **hibernate** in winter. They sleep in dens, or holes, underground. Most garter snakes use the same den every year. Thousands of snakes can share the same den.

◄ Grassy lawns are one of garter snakes' many habitats.

What Garter Snakes Eat

Garter snakes hunt small prey. They eat insects, earthworms, frogs, toads, and salamanders. Some large garter snakes eat mice.

Garter snakes do not have long fangs or deadly venom. They must catch and hold their prey. Garter snakes start swallowing the prey as soon as they catch it. The prey is swallowed alive while it is still struggling to get away.

◄ Garter snakes eat insects, such as grasshoppers.

Life Cycle of a Garter Snake

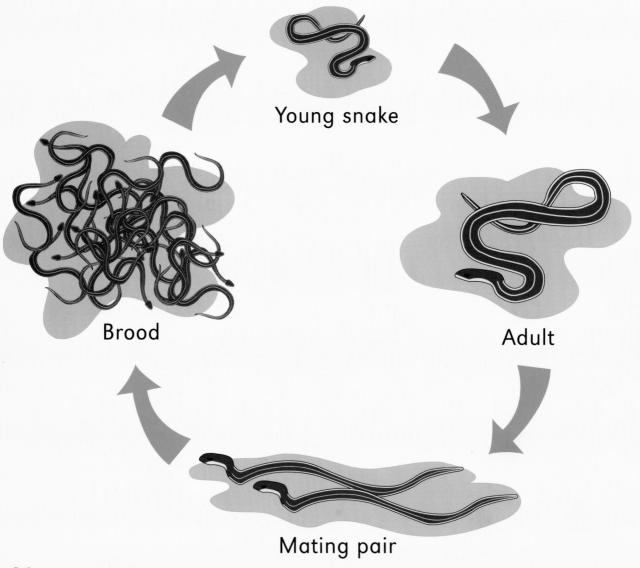

Young snake

Adult

Mating pair

Brood

Producing Young

Garter snakes usually **mate** during spring. In colder areas, the snakes usually mate right after hibernating. Often many male snakes try to mate with the same female. They form large groups called mating balls.

The female carries her young inside her body. The young snakes grow in thin egg sacs. In late summer, the female gives birth. Most females give birth to 10 to 30 young. A group of young snakes is called a brood.

Growing Up

Female garter snakes do not care for their young. Garter snakes have to take care of themselves as soon as they are born.

Young garter snakes look like small adults. They are 7.5 to 9 inches (19 to 23 centimeters) long at birth. Most young garter snakes do not live to be adults. Many of them are eaten by other animals.

Garter snakes shed their skin, or **molt**, as they grow. They loosen their old skin on rocks or logs. Then they crawl out of the old skin.

◀ A garter snake's colors are bright right after molting.

Dangers to Garter Snakes

Many **predators** eat garter snakes. Birds, such as hawks and owls, hunt garter snakes. Foxes and raccoons also eat them. Even house cats kill many garter snakes.

Garter snakes are good at **adapting** to new environments. They live near people without too much trouble. Adapting helps them be one of the most common reptiles in North America.

◄ A hawk makes a quick meal out of a young garter snake. Many garter snakes do not live to be adults.

Amazing Facts about Garter Snakes

- Some garter snake dens hold more than 10,000 hibernating snakes. In Canada, people can go on snake watching tours near large dens in spring.

- Garter snakes can release a smelly, bad-tasting fluid, called **musk**. Most animals will drop a garter snake as soon as it releases its musk.

- Garter snakes are the only wild snake ever seen in the U.S. state of Alaska.

◄ Garter snakes leave their den at the same time. Males watch for females who may want to mate.

Glossary

adapt (uh-DAPT)—to adjust to a new situation or environment

cold-blooded (KOHLD-BLUHD-id)—having a body temperature that is the same as the surroundings; all reptiles are cold-blooded.

hibernate (HYE-bur-nate)—to spend the winter in a deep sleep

mate (MATE)—join together to produce young

molt (MOHLT)—to shed an outer layer of skin

musk (MUHSK)—an oily, strong-smelling fluid

predator (PRED-uh-tur)—an animal that hunts other animals for food

prey (PRAY)—an animal that is hunted for food

venom (VEN-uhm)—a poisonous liquid made by some snakes; snakes inject venom into prey through hollow fangs.

Read More

Stille, Darlene R. *Snakes.* First Reports. Minneapolis: Compass Point Books, 2001.

Wechsler, Doug. *Garter Snakes.* The Really Wild Life of Snakes. New York: PowerKids Press, 2001.

Internet Sites

FactHound offers a safe, fun way to find Internet sites related to this book. All of the sites on FactHound have been researched by our staff.

Here's how:
1. Visit *www.facthound.com*
2. Type in this special code **0736837329** for age-appropriate sites. Or enter a search word related to this book for a more general search.
3. Click on the **Fetch It** button.

FactHound will fetch the best sites for you!

Index